MOUNTAIN MEADOWS...OCEAN MEADOWS

Yosemite -- Bend -- Portland -- Oregon Coast -- San Francisco

Charles Anderson

Charles Anderson

Copyright © 2nd Edition July 14, 2022 Charles Anderson

www.travelsonourown.com

All rights reserved.

This book is a nonfiction travelogue.

No part of this book may be reproduced, or stored in a retrieval system, or transmitted in any form or by any means, electronic, mechanical, photocopying, recording, or otherwise, without express written permission of the publisher.

ISBN Paperback Edition: 9798841654681

Cover design by: Charles Anderson
Printed in the United States of America

PREFACE

The inspiration for this road trip was an obligation to visit our daughter in Portland. Being from southern California, this provided an opportunity to travel into new heretofore unexplored territories. Although, having traveled to Big Sur, San Francisco, Napa, the Sierra Nevada up to Lake Tahoe, visiting Yosemite was an entirely new adventure and the Tioga Road linking Yosemite Valley to Rte. 395 along the flank of the Sierra Nevada provided a convenient path through Nevada to high-desert northeast California and a track via Bend, Oregon to Portland. The return itinerary included three overnights on the Oregon Coast: Cannon Beach, Newport and Bandon. While the Oregon coast is not as severe or wild as Big Sur it certainly has no shortage of natural wonders and recreational destinations. The coast has 22 major estuaries that play a vital role in the ecological and economic health of the coast and the entire state. These estuaries offer a gentle topography in contrast to the elevated and forested land formations that alternate between the ocean inlets and small population centers. Whereas Yosemite and the Tioga Road were the early highlights of the trip, the sights of tidal waters penetrating inland, well-tended, cultivated and open wild meadows and wetland features and critters remain very distinct in my memory. The pre-trip photography theme was mountain meadows and ocean meadows. Hopefully, what follows delivers on this initial plan. The last, first-time destination was the State and National Redwood Parks between Crescent City and Eureka, California with an overnight in Eureka. These old growth specimens did not disappoint. The remainder of the trip via San Francisco provided a re-acquaintance with the city but was otherwise pro forma other than the surprise passage along the South Fork of the Eel River which the locals would probably prefer to keep to themselves.

CHARLES ANDERSON

This road trip of less than two weeks was, with some overnight exceptions and leisurely sampling of the foodie establishments on Division Street in southeast Portland, a drive-by exercise, especially the runs from Mono Lake to Susanville and Susanville to Bend. Hopefully, the chronicle does not read like a blur and the photos flesh out the highlights. The one unanticipated drawback was the fog, smoke and rain on the Oregon Coast that either eliminated altogether a handful of worthy potential visuals or affected the illumination for some of those included herein. Enjoy.

AUGUST 29, 2017: YOSEMITE

Jumped off from Newport Beach with miniature schnauzer, Francine, peering out the back seat window. Took the I-405 to the I-5 and once down the Grape Vine we split off onto CA-99. Its 100+ degrees outside as we speed past miles and miles of agribusinesses, the economic engines that power California's Central Valley. Groves, vineyards, grain fields, fallow and uncultivated acreage extend to the horizon while service vehicles stir up clouds of dust. The drive reveals a tableau of engaged field hands, service pickup trucks, produce-laden big rigs, heavy equipment purveyors, processing plants and grain elevators. Bakersfield, Delano, Visalia and Fresno. Fresno has a big city vibrant look of prosperity and growth compared to its contemporaries. Turning north northeast onto CA-41, the Sierra's loom in the distance. As we approach the foothills there is a huge plume of smoke dead ahead coming from a forest fire at the Fish Camp about 15 miles southeast of Yosemite Valley. The plume initially generates some anxiety. We take CA-49 to CA-140 and, then, follow the Merced River Gorge to El Portal.

Around 3:30 pm we arrive at our accommodations, Yosemite View Lodge, it is located alongside the Merced Gorge and is replete with a restaurant and four swimming pools located a mile from the Arch Rock Entrance to the park. After checking-in, we head to the park. First stop at the western end of the valley floor are the spectacles of Bridalveil Fall to the south and El Capitan to the north. The fall stands just over 600 feet above the valley floor. As the water courses over the cataract and descends the rock face it produces a mist resembling a veil which early natives regarded as spiritual.

Bridalveil Fall

El Capitan, a glacial creation, is a granite monolith that extends 3,000 feet from its base to summit. Its grand sheer face immediately grabs one's attention and imagination. It commands the valley, hence, the name El Capitan. Climbers flock from around the world to gain its summit from the dare-devils who scale its face to the recreational hiker who treks the trail to its summit from Yosemite Falls.

El Capitan Framed

Upon seeing El Capitan one easily comprehends why Ansel Adams repeatedly since his boyhood returned to Yosemite to capture its majesty. Its pale, flinty-gray, striated face bordered in green along its base by both leafy and conifer trees furnish a favorite setting for amateur and professional photographers. It is a popular subject for photo studies of variations in light and season. Today the light is muted by the smoke cloud arising from the Fish Camp fire.

El Capitan Zoomed In

We continue east on Southside Drive along the valley floor to the Four Mile Trailhead. Sentinel Dome is to our right and lush meadows astride the Merced River are on our left. Sentinel Dome is a granite dome with an elevation gain of about 550 feet from the Taft Point Trailhead. The trail to the popular summit is a moderate hike made all the more worthwhile because of its spectacular 360 degree view for miles and miles of the Valley.

Sentinel Dome

It is late afternoon and there are lots of park visitors about. Some are strolling, biking or skateboarding along the roadway. Others, either setting out or returning, are congregating at the trailheads.

Tour buses and wagons are at capacity. The swimmers, canoers, and fishermen are active in the quiet waters of the Merced whereas sunbathers or loungers occupy its lawns and banks. The atmosphere is a mix of and active outdoor laid back types.

Sentinel Meadow 1

The sponge-like "Montane" meadows bounded by tree stands are lush from the spring flow and shallow ground water of the Merced. The grasses are bright green, thick and several feet in length. Boardwalk trails have been constructed to crisscross the meadows to guide visitors and reduce haphazard foot traffic from trampling the grasses. Wildlife that feed and breed in the meadow include mule deer, coyotes, ground squirrels, gophers, frogs, salamanders, willow flycatchers and butterflies. Flora includes wild flowers and rare orchid species. These graceful green grasslands represent epitomes of vast mountain meadows.

Sentinel Meadow 2

The Yosemite Valley Chapel is nestled next to the trailhead in a natural setting among towering sequoias. Built in the 1870's, this picturesque wooden structure has been moved several times, the last because of flooding to its foundation. Its simple Carpenter Gothic design and paint work give it (to me) a Scandinavian feel. The chapel serves as an active house of worship and wedding venue for locals and park visitors.

Yosemite Valley Chapel

Continuing on we encounter Half Dome which looms 5,000 feet from the valley floor at the eastern end of the valley. It is an icon with a popular, 12-hour roundtrip hiking trail that leads to its summit. The last 400 feet are negotiated via a parallel double cable system requiring some nerve, strength, good health and a permit. The hike is very challenging and requires preparation. The rock formation is named for its shape which is an imposing sheer face oriented towards the valley and a smoothly contoured dome forming its other three sides.

Half Dome

Following the auto circuit towards the Visitor Center, we happen upon another remarkable golden-grass meadow with a contrasting green border of tree stands below the Yosemite Falls. The Falls, one of the world's tallest, drop about 2,500 feet and are composed of three separate falls. The Falls are deafening in the spring and summer when the winter runoff is peaking. There is a short (1 mile) and easy hiking trail (1,000 feet of elevation) to Columbia Rock to view the upper and lower cascading spectacles and the meadows below.

Yosemite Falls

We drive by the iconic Ahwahnee Hotel where late arrivals are unloading their baggage and outdoor gear. It's nearing twilight but the air remains toasty. There remain outdoors lots of hikers hustling to beat the darkness and visitors meandering about. Clearly, Yosemite garners an immense audience of nature lovers. The views are imposing and the sense of grandeur settles into one's psyche. For now, we have pretty much covered the Valley highlights so we wrap it up in order to return to our lodge. Along the way, the two-lane traffic becomes snarled as parkgoers abandon their cars in droves to glimpse and photograph a bear swimming midstream in the Merced. Shortly, a park ranger arrives and angrily breaks up the gawkers.

Back at our accommodations, we leisurely dine on the resort restaurant's string-lit patio while regarding ten yards distant the moderate flow of the Merced over shallow rocks. This tranquil ambiance is momentarily broken by Francine's barking at our waiter. Quiet girl!

Tenaya Creek Meadow

AUGUST 30, 2017: YOSEMITE'S TIOGA HIGHWAY TRAIL TO LEE VINING, MONO LAKE AND CA RTE. 395 VIA RENO, NV TO SUSANVILLE, CA.

An early morning pall of smoke from the Fish Camp fire hangs in the Merced Gorge. It is uncomfortably heavy for an asthma sufferer so we break camp early. We head into the park and ascend the Big Oak Flat Road to connect to Tioga Road which crosses the Yosemite Sierra and runs about 60 miles east to Mono Lake and Lee Vining. There has been a brief shower and in no time the air clears and freshens. We ascend to a ridge line and begin a winding tour through deeply wooded forests where sunlight sometimes barely penetrates. The pavement is wet and thick ferns cover the forest floor. From time to time the forest opens and we are atop heights viewing a panorama of Yosemite summits.

White Wolf

As we emerge from the more deep-forested range of the western portion of the Tioga Road, the vistas almost rival those of the Grand Canyon. Granite domes soar and in rounding turns we plunge into mile long ravines that bottom out as either pristine meadows or lakes. About half way along we reach Olmsted Point, a harsh, wind-swept lunar landscape of denuded granite and solitary fir trees rooted in the rock crevices. The surrounding rock formations are abuzz with scatterings of visitors gleefully exploring this alien terrain.

Olmstead Point 1

In addition to the fascinating glacial erratic, granite boulder fields, Olmstead Point provides a very scenic view to the southwest as Half Dome looms about 2-1/2 miles in the distance. During our stop, a park volunteer has mounted a telescope and positioned it for viewing the ant-like clusters of hearty hikers on Half Dome. This lookout point is a must and offers a very spacious parking area just off Tioga Road via an easy turnout. It comfortably accommodates caravans of buses and cars.

Half Dome from Olmstead Point

Descending rapidly from Olmstead Point, we bottom out at Tenaya Lake. It's a stunning alpine lake at an elevation of 8,150 feet surrounded by granite domes and lodge-pole trees. It is considered a visual jewel by many but today it lacks its usual shimmering beauty because the light is defused by smoke and clouds. As it sits conveniently and immediately southeast of the roadway, it is a popular summer venue for trout fishing, canoeing, kayaking, swimming, picknicking and sunbathing. We didn't see any bears but they are common visitors.

Tenaya Lake

We stop for a quick look around and out of necessity we must use the primitive toilet facilities just beyond the lake which challenge both our senses and soft-living sensitivities. Blessedly, Tuolumne Peak is just opposite the parking lot and we are rewarded with the view of an extraordinarily picturesque stand of foxtail pine trees cradled just below the summit with their glossy, verdant, bottle-brush foliage backlit by a wall of bright white granite.

Tuolumne Peak

A mile further on we enter Tuolumne Meadows where the Tuolumne River gently meanders through a broad mostly grassy plain punctuated with exposed glaciated granite. The meadows in contrast to the peaks and domes of Yosemite have a serene rather than stunning natural beauty. This area was a spiritual and revered hunting ground coveted by its early native inhabitants. The meadows are sub-alpine at 8,500 feet and seasonally flooded by the spring snow thaw. This hydrology supports a vast variety of fauna and flora. Six plant communities consisting principally of sedges and alpine aster inhabit the meadows.

Tuolumne Meadow Looking North

We turnoff Tioga Road into a campground parking lot and, crossing the road, walk through the meadow towards the river where there remain a few wild flowers blooming in the river jack. The meadow is a mosaic of wet, moist and dry ground supporting different habitats. All about are burrow mounds. The meadow provides a prodigious habitat for deer, ground squirrels, pocket gophers and other small mammals.

Tuolumne Meadow Flora

Closer to the river one finds alpine drift wood, river jack deposits and other evidence of the annual flooding accompanying winter snowpack thaw that nourishes the meadow's vegetation. In the 19th century herders grazed sheep on these meadows until the practice was no longer economically feasible and was entirely abandoned.

Tuolumne Meadow Driftwood

The pristine river, more a big stream in the meadow, is fairly narrow and shallow and inviting. River jack deposits litter the river shallows, its banks and the meadow. Small sandy beaches are formed at the inner curves of the river and are perfect recreation spots for picnicking and exploring.

Tuolumne River

Tuolumne Meadows has a large but quite basic-amenity campsite, a bare-bones lodge for glampers, a store and post office. It is a very popular draw for hiking, rock climbing, backpacking and fishing. Like all of Yosemite there are bears about.

Mt Dana Meadow

Back on the road but close by, Mt. Dana, still sporting some snowpack residue, serves as a backdrop for an isolated alpine meadow.

Even further along and just south of the Gaylor Lake Trailhead, Mt. Dana again serves as a backdrop for a pristine alpine meadow framing a small lake.

Mt Dana Alpine Lake

We are now approaching Tioga Pass and the views are wide-screen and more grandiose. We hurtle down the highway to Tioga Lake and then Ellery Lake and on to Tioga Pass.

Tioga Peak at 11,526 feet is an enormous prominence, a mostly-bald, granite structure with scree fields measuring over 1,000 feet or so sweeping down its flanks.

Lake Tioga

Lake Tioga is a small glacial lake at an elevation of 9,700 feet. There are limited camp sites with easy access to fishing, hiking, rock climbing, bird watching, photography and wild flower viewing. It is prefered by those who avoid the crowds of Yosemite Valley and pure nature lovers. Weather is unpredictable.

Tioga Peak

After the Tioga Pass we are now heading for the exit at the eastern end of the park, we are losing elevation in a g-force fashion. On our right is a large, sunken valley meadow, Horses Meadow, with a cluster of campsites along the Lee Vining Creek. Mono Lake is dead ahead. Several more miles and we stop at the intersection of CA Rte. 395, a short distance below the tiny, staging hamlet of Lee Vining which sits on the boundary of the Sierra Nevada and the Great Basin.

Horses Meadow Lee Vining Creek

About a mile north on Rte. 395 is the Mono Lake Tufa State Natural Reserve, a scenic area for exploring the wonders of the lake. Mono Lake is a large, desert lake with no outlet at the western extreme of the Great Basin of the Western U.S. It is 13 miles long and 9 miles wide. Runoff generated from the snowpack of surrounding elevations delivers high salt concentrations which gives the lake a very high salinity. The spectacular example of this salinity is the stand of "tufa" towers at the southern end of the lake. Tufa is a limestone formation arising from a chemical reaction of calcium carbonate accumulating with the seasonal variances in the the lake's water level.

Mono Lake Tufa

It is about noon and our leg for the remainder of the day is to drive to Susanville, CA, via Carson City and Reno, NV. Leaving Mono Lake we head north towards Bridgeport, CA. Descending into Bridgeport at 6,500 feet there is an immense mountain meadow crisscrossed with streams and blanketed with lush grasses irrigated by snowpack flows. The meadow supports commercial large-scale cattle ranching and extends for miles. Bridgeport with a population of less than 600 enjoys a year round tourism industry with a wide range of activities for the outdoor enthusiast: dude ranches, fishing; a large reservoir for water sports; trekking, hiking, mountain climbing and backpacking and in the winter snowmobiling, cross-county skiing and snowshoeing.

Big Meadow Bridgeport

Bridgeport is the County Seat of Mono County and had a brief moment of celebrity-hood in 1947. It served for some on-location filming for the Hollywood production of, "Out of the Past", featuring Kirk Douglas and Robert Mitchum. Several close-up shots included the quaint Victorian Mono County Court House, the pride of Bridgeport.

Mono County Court House

As we approached the Nevada border south of Topaz Lake there was another forest fire billowing plumes of smoke skyward. Flames were visible on the ridges above Slinkard Valley. As we crossed the Nevada line, the Highway Patrol was closing Rte. 395. In another minute we would have been forced to return to Bridgeport. Being spared a forced reversal of course we cruised along past Carson City and onto a new bypass east of Reno. Reno has a skyline marked by high-rise office buildings and casinos. With a population of about 250,000 it appears to be an economic success story and in the midst a hyper growth phase. As it turns out Reno would have been a more entertaining alternative than Susanville.

Two hours north of Reno we reach Susanville. Along the way, having begun at Mono Lake we are skirting the western limits of the Great Basin and northern limits of the Sierra Nevada. The topography is mostly high desert composed of wide valleys bordered by mountain ranges which form a giant closed-watershed where precipitation either evaporates, collects in basins or sinks below the surface since there is no outflow. We observe a vast open range of grass lands and scrub with cattle and sheep grazing, occasional feed lots and, as far as the eye can see, meadows of hay cultivation. Along the way we pass alongside for 6 miles or more, Honey Lake, an immense collection basin which is flooded, muddy, rippling in the wind with no distinct shoreline and devoid of any human improvements or signs of recreational activity. We had encountered a number of these shallow lakes (e.g., Washoe Lake north of Carson), some quite large, on our journey still brimming with last winter's heavy precipitation.

Susanville and its downtown commercial district are a bit drab as its core industry of timber production and milling have long since departed. Once a stopover and rail junction for migrants following the Oregon Trail its glory days are in the past. Today, it relies on a nearby U.S. Army Depot (the 15-square-mile Sierra Army Depot brimming with magazine storages and combat vehicle parks), two California prisons and a Federal prison at Herlong to bolster its economy.

We enjoyed our lodging at the Roseberry House Bed and Breakfast near the town's Masonic Temple in a neighborhood where wild deer wander and munch on flowers and landscaping with impunity. Moreover, the deer population is considerable and appears to be mounting because of unrestrained growth.

Susanville Masonic Lodge

AUGUST 31, 2017: SUSANVILLE TO BEND, OREGON VIA KLAMATH FALLS, OREGON.

It is cool but very smoky with hazy yellow skies as we climb a crumbling two-lane CA Rte. 139 heading toward Klamath Falls. We travel for several hours through some sparsely populated territory with minimal highway traffic. Meanwhile the location and status of forest fires are a concern.

We pass Eagle Lake which appears to have a stable enough water level to support lakeside housing and water recreation. We move along in and out of large stretches of range lands and timber stands much of it within the Modoc National Forest. It is a bit lonely. There are cattle ranches and hay farms to occasionally break the monotonous landscape. We are keeping an eye out for a picturesque barn or outbuilding to photograph but there is nothing out of the ordinary until we reach Adin, a hamlet of 271 inhabitants. Finally, we are blessed by a structure of the Triple-J Ranch, an old barn festooned with a new roof and an extended roofline sheltering two vintage, horse-drawn buggies.

Adin's Triple–J Ranch Barn

Crossing into Oregon the surroundings take on a different tone. The open range gives way to intense cultivation where potatoes appear to be the main cash crop. Potato storage barns are a visual curiosity as they are built half buried into the ground to maintain a low-light environment for the harvested potatoes. Stopping to refuel we are mildly amused when an attendant stepped out to pump gasoline. As he chatted, the young man in street clothes continued to work his earwax with the butt end of the lanyard holding the keys that unlock the gas pump. I didn't fully realize at the time, that by state law, only authorized gas station employees were permitted to pump gas. Welcome to Oregon.

Next stop is Klamath Falls, a lumber industry town of 20,000 situated on the southeastern shore of Upper Klamath Lake settled in the 1860's while historically inhabited by the Klamath and Modoc people. We pass through the old town which looks pretty chipper and appears bent on preserving an aging but well-maintained old town commercial base. We drive to the Visitor's Center seeking directions to the "Falls". Apparently, they are a bit out of the way and since we had a dinner date in Bend, we reluctantly passed up the tour opportunity.

On OR Rte. 97 it is a straight shot of several-hours north to Bend. Just out of town the Upper Klamath Lake extends for 25 miles. It is drained by the Klamath River and has for decades been a battleground pitting farmers against environmentalists. The route to Bend is bounded by forest lands with small hamlets along the way and signs announcing dozens of popular camping sites and points of interest. Crater Lake National Park lies to the west and at one point the lake itself is just an alluring 10 miles away. To the east is Winema National Forest and Klamath Marsh National Wildlife Refuge.

We reach Bend about 4:00 pm. As we approach the center of town we notice a lot of newly-constructed commercial buildings evidencing that Bend is bustling due greatly to its environs which are super popular for retirees, tourists and outdoor enthusiasts. Our Day's Inn accommodations are easily accessed, adequate and convenient to downtown. We have a dinner date with a couple who are good friends with our daughter and her husband. Just before twilight, we meet for dinner on the patio at "Barrio" which looks out on Drake Park and Mirror Pond. Our host is a manager. The company is convivial and the food (Latin American --- meaning lots and lots of chilies) and drink were appetizing and festive: grilled-pineapple mescal cocktail, paella, calamari, grilled green beans, and Brussels+bacon+bluecheese, …voila!

SEPTEMBER 1, 2017: BEND TO PORTLAND VIA MT HOOD.

Distant forest fires are active and the air is acrid.

We head downtown to Mirror Lake for some photography. The lake is formed by damming the Deschutes River and provides a picturesque setting of lakeside homes opposite Drake Park. The park and its lawn extending from the old town center are a popular gathering place in the center of town. Surrounded by craft breweries and eateries, it's a magnet for both families and the young crowd.

Mirror Pond at Drake Park

Pine Tavern Old Town Bend

We mosey over to a cafe, La Magie Bakery, for enhanced coffees and pastry. On the way we purchase matching "Eclipse 2017" tee shirts. Afterwards, we depart for Portland.

Our tight itinerary did not afford any in-depth exploration of Bend beyond our wonderful dinner and morning stroll in Bend. My understanding is that Bend is an oasis lying on the eastern slope of the Cascade Range and a paradise for the outdoor enthusiast and retiree as evidenced by its doubling population.

Tourism is a major force in Bend's economy. It is growing by leaps and bounds and is a mecca for all sorts of recreational activity, including golf. Mt Bachelor is a popular ski area with 10 lifts just 12 miles west of town. The spectacular 250-mile Deschutes River which is dammed to form Mirror Pond drains the Cascades and flows north to the Columbia River. It supports a great deal of water recreation, camping, fishing and white-water rafting.

Now dormant, the area contains a number of volcanic points of interest including an extinct volcano within the city limits and lava formations such as the Lava River Cave south of town. Tumalo State Park just 4 miles from Bend on the Deschutes is a popular getaway especially for the locals.

There is an active forest fire in Sisters to the northwest fouling the air as we follow OR Rte. 97 towards Mt Hood. We drive through the scrubby high desert until Madras where we turn west of OR Rte. 26 and head into the ponderosa pine forests of the Cascades.

Mt Hood

Around noon we exit OR Rte. 26 and wind up the Timberline Highway to the Timberline Lodge and trailheads of Mt Hood. We are on the south face of the mountain and it is radiant and hot. We are at the upper end of the timberline at 6,000 feet and there are snow-packs remaining above 8,000 feet. The parking lot for late summer is quite full with pockets of hardy, die-hard skiers coming and going. There are small collections of visitors checking out the lodge but we conclude that most of the parking lot occupants are hiking the multitude of trails, which lace this enormous mountain with a summit of 11,240 feet. Mt Hood is potentially volcanic, has 12 glaciers (snow fields) and is regularly subject to swarms of seismic activity. It supports six ski areas, hiking and technical mountain climbing. Just 50 miles southeast and visible from Portland, the mountain is a gigantic recreation draw for the state.

The Timberline Lodge is a National Historic Landmark completed in 1938 as part of a WPA project. It attracts 2 million visitors a year and appeared in the opening footage of Hollywood's "The Shining".

Timberline Lodge

We depart Mt. Hood for the final leg of our journey to Portland. We arrive mid-afternoon close to our destination in southeast Portland but initially confused by the street numbering system we end up in Woodstock rather than Darlington. Recovering nicely, in another 10 minutes we pull into our hosts' driveway.

After an extended greeting and as the outside temperature is cooling somewhat we drive over for dinner to the Sellwood-Moreland district which is a genuine foody haven. Our hosts insist on patronizing, "a Cena Ristorante". It is an intimate, cozy Italian trattoria serving yummy pasta creations. The dinner menu changes frequently but we had the lobster with corn and mascarpone agnolotti, giardiniera pickled vegetables and eggplant parmigiana, superb dining along with some bold red wines. After our bon repas, we return to the Chateau Gounier.

SEPTEMBER 2, 2017: PORTLAND

It is sunny, warm and a little smoky. For breakfast we pick up some house-made pastries at Mehri's Bakery and Cafe, a quaint bakery and breakfast stop on SE 52nd Avenue.

By late morning we hop over to Mt. Tabor, a volcanic cinder cone, for sightseeing and a short hike. Mt. Tabor with a 600+ foot summit is an extinct volcano centrally located in the South East Quarter of Portland. The name comes from Mt. Tabor in Israel which is a historic site from antiquity just 6 miles from Nazareth and which has a comparable volcanic dome topography. It is a park with extensive hiking paths and three reservoirs. There are plenty of trees with broad canopy which makes for a cool environment. From the west side of the park there is a commanding view down Hawthorne Boulevard and across the Willamette River bridges to downtown Portland.

Downtown Portland: Koin and Wells Fargo Centers

Looking a little further to the southwest the dramatic Tilikum Bridge is eye-catching. This suspension, cable-stayed bridge with double pyramid towers carries exclusively light-rail, buses, bicycles and pedestrians. The shape of the towers mimics the profile of Mt. Hood which is visible from downtown Portland. We descend Mt. Tabor by car to Division Street to partake in the Saturday hubbub of commercial street life in the Richmond neighborhood. Division Street houses Portland's renowned restaurant row. Between 30th and 51st blocks there are three dozen eateries and bars with some pot shops thrown in to boot. There are plenty of boutiques and retail as well. Also, very noticeable is what appears to be a surge of new, low-rise, Bauhaus-like design, residential construction replete with convenient retail space at street level. Very hip.

Tilikum Bridge

In the early evening we return to Division Street and Woodsman's Tavern with the express goal of having our host for the first time consume some raw oysters. We were successful but it will take more than one oyster to convert him. The oyster lovers finished off several dozen and enjoyed crab and prawn Louie along with several rounds of cocktails. The tavern, serving an American menu, possesses a comfortable, laid-back atmosphere with good food and service, not too fancy but welcoming.

We return to the residence and gather on the patio. The smoke has intensified. It turns out that earlier around 4:00 pm a 14-year-old had tossed a pyrotechnic into dry brush at Eagle Creek Trailhead, a popular hiking area for locals, just astride the Columbia River about 40 miles east of Portland. The fire rapidly spread to 3,000 acres and eventually over the next two weeks it will grow to 50,000. For the moment the smoke has converted the sun into a harmless to the eyes rose ball. Cocktail and music and Cajun storytelling time, all provided by the host.

Smokey Twilight

Looking a little further to the southwest the dramatic Tilikum Bridge is eye-catching. This suspension, cable-stayed bridge with double pyramid towers carries exclusively light-rail, buses, bicycles and pedestrians. The shape of the towers mimics the profile of Mt. Hood which is visible from downtown Portland. We descend Mt. Tabor by car to Division Street to partake in the Saturday hubbub of commercial street life in the Richmond neighborhood. Division Street houses Portland's renowned restaurant row. Between 30th and 51st blocks there are three dozen eateries and bars with some pot shops thrown in to boot. There are plenty of boutiques and retail as well. Also, very noticeable is what appears to be a surge of new, low-rise, Bauhaus-like design, residential construction replete with convenient retail space at street level. Very hip.

Tilikum Bridge

In the early evening we return to Division Street and Woodsman's Tavern with the express goal of having our host for the first time consume some raw oysters. We were successful but it will take more than one oyster to convert him. The oyster lovers finished off several dozen and enjoyed crab and prawn Louie along with several rounds of cocktails. The tavern, serving an American menu, possesses a comfortable, laid-back atmosphere with good food and service, not too fancy but welcoming.

We return to the residence and gather on the patio. The smoke has intensified. It turns out that earlier around 4:00 pm a 14-year-old had tossed a pyrotechnic into dry brush at Eagle Creek Trailhead, a popular hiking area for locals, just astride the Columbia River about 40 miles east of Portland. The fire rapidly spread to 3,000 acres and eventually over the next two weeks it will grow to 50,000. For the moment the smoke has converted the sun into a harmless to the eyes rose ball. Cocktail and music and Cajun storytelling time, all provided by the host.

Smokey Twilight

SEPTEMBER 3, 2017: PORTLAND

It is still warm and very smoky with ash from the Eagle Creek fire accumulating like snow on the driveway, decks and autos.

We drive to Vancouver, WA, on a shopping errand and then return to drive by Kelly Point Park and the Pearcy Island Marine Terminal. The area serves as both a public park and a major port facility for handling, storing and redirecting transport of ocean-going shipping traffic. Kelley Point is the northern tip of Pearcy Island which is formed by the Willamette River to the west, the Columbia River to the north and the Columbia Sough to the south. We pass through the town of St. Johns and crossover the Willamette on the iconic St. Johns Bridge, a steel suspension bridge with dual gothic towers, the tallest in Portland, circa 1931.

After cruising the neighborhoods in the west hills of Portland, we park at Hoyt Arboretum and hike the trails down to the Archery Range and back. The arboretum contains about 6,000 trees made up of 2,000 species of which many are identified by labels with both their scientific and common names. There is a multitude of Japanese hollies on the trail adjacent to the parking lot. The walk is hearty with deep, cool woods and significant elevation changes on the narrow trails.

Hoyt Arboretum

There are plenty of other hikers in small groups, many maintaining a jogging pace and others accompanied by their eager and exhilarated, tongue drooping canine companions. It is refreshing to be outdoors as the smoky atmosphere has let up some for the moment.

Trailside Bloomer

We return to the residence for a hearty community prepared repast featuring a borlotti bean salad with anchovies and mozzarella cheese.

SEPTEMBER 4, 2017: ASTORIA, FORT STEVENS AND CANNON BEACH

We depart Portland for the coast. Navigating the late morning, rush hour traffic on the Westside of Portland was a little tricky but we ultimately merge onto the US Rte. 26 and speed off towards Cannon Beach. We flash by suburbs, farms and then deep timberland. In less than two hours we reach US Rte. 101 at the coast. It is early so we drive north on to explore Astoria.

Astoria (population 10,000), settled as a fur trading post in 1811 close to an earlier encampment of Lewis and Clark dating from 1805-06, sits at the southern shore of the mouth of the Columbia River where it enters the Pacific Ocean. Its namesake is John Jacob Astor a New York investor whose American Fur Company founded Fort Astoria. It was the first American settlement west of the Rockies. The ancient Clatsop indian tribe inhabited the Astoria area for thousands of years before the 1811 settlements were founded.

Astoria is connected to the neighboring shore of Washington State via the 4-mile Astoria-Megler Bridge built in 1966. Astoria has a long history as a deepwater port of entry. In the past it relied on fishing, fish processing plants and lumber all of which have ceased meaningful operations because of competition, regulation and declines of species and habitat shifts in fish populations. Today there is a shift to tourism with a riverfront trolley and an influx of brew pubs and restaurants along its waterfront. The Columbia River Maritime Museum serves as a focal point for tourists, showcasing fishing, shipping and military history and a mooring for several cruise ship lines and the excursion riverboat, American Empress.

American Empress

Columbia River Lightship

Other Astoria points of interest include the late 19th century Capt. George Flavel House, a Victorian gem which is now a museum. Flavel was a riverboat pilot and prominent Astoria businessman. For popular culture and entertainment, just across the street from the Flavel House is the former Clatsop County Jail which is now the Oregon Film Museum housing memorabilia and promoting films (Goonies, The Black Stallion, Short Circuit) featuring Astoria locations. Lastly, there is the Astoria Tower built in 1926 overlooking the mouth of the Columbia River. Standing 125 feet, it is patterned after the Place Vendome Column in Paris and was financed by the Astors.

MOUNTAIN MEADOWS...OCEAN MEADOWS

Flavel House

Clatsop County Jail

Upon leaving Astoria for Cannon Beach, we made a short side trip to Ft. Stevens, a shore artillery emplacement dating from the U.S. Civil War which defended the mouth of the Columbia River against foreign warships. It was decommissioned in 1947 and ultimately ceded to the Oregon Parks and Recreation Department.

In 1942 a Japanese submarine shelled the fort but only succeeded in slightly damaging the backstop at the baseball field.

Ft Stevens Howitzer

Finally arriving in Cannon Beach a popular Portland, year round getaway, we stroll back and forth through the shopping district of the compact shore side village which lies just two blocks from the beach. Its name was inspired by a cannon from a 19th century US Navy schooner (Shark) that grounded on the Columbia Bar ("Graveyard of the Pacific") in 1846. The cannon was rediscovered in 1898.

Cannon Beach is upscale and quaint with mostly single and two-story, gray-green shingled exteriors and white trim giving a Cape Cod feel to the town. We browse the dress shops, boutiques, art galleries, ice creameries, cafes and candy kitchens before purchasing several bottles of Oregon pinot noir at Laurel's Wine shop.

Steidel's Art Gallery Cannon Beach

Our lodging is several miles south at the Tolovana Inn which sits immediately on the beach. The accommodations and setting adjacent to the Tolovana Beach State Recreation Site are quite pleasant. We re-provision across the highway at the Fresh Foods organic grocery then check-in, relax and, after twilight, return downtown Cannon Beach for dinner at the Driftwood Inn. We dine al fresco on the patio as Francine isn't allowed in the interior dining areas. The food and wine are appetizing and the outdoor ambiance makes for a pleasant evening at the shore.

SEPTEMBER 6, 2017: CANNON BEACH, MANZANITA, TILLAMOOK AND NEWPORT

After coffee and Danish, we hike the beach a mile north to Haystack Rock which is featured in the opening and closing scenes of the 1985 movie, "Goonies".

Haystack Rock

We count three resort hotels along the ocean front. The seaside community includes single-family residences numbering in the hundreds between Rte. 101 and the low bluffs bordering the beach. Cedar shake shingles and white trim are the order of the day.

The thick fog limits photography to close-ups. Haystack Rock is one of the more recognizable land formations on the Oregon

Coast. It extends vertically 235 feet from the ocean floor but is accessible by foot at low tide. Its environs include several other shorter basalt formations and tidal pools with all sorts of attendant marine life. It is also a sanctuary for nesting seabirds such as puffins and terns. The marine life and seabirds are protected under Oregon law with no collecting of specimens and access to the rock itself above the barnacle line is prohibited. Given the weather conditions, not surprisingly there are no large tourist throngs about this morning so we move about unimpeded.

For Francine this is a gigantic dog park with water, sand, beach debris and aloof seabirds just begging to be chased by a fool barking dog. It should be noted that an emergency vehicle is parked just beyond the waterline as visitors are occasionally trapped by the incoming tide à la Mont Saint Michel in France and require rescue.

The fog mixed with some forest fire smoke is uncooperative and it is cool enough to necessitate long pants and jackets so we wrap it up and motor south to Newport.

Tide Pools at Haystack Rock

The geography of the Oregon Coast includes large stretches of wide beaches and sloughs, ocean and bay meadows, elevated headlands with spectacular ocean views of landfalls and surf, basalt stacks situated along the beach or poking from the ocean, and several dozen estuaries some with large bays which penetrate inland to locations suitable for developing the larger settlements along the coast (e.g., Tillamook and Coos Bay). There are many vista points and points of interest such as lighthouses and capes along this 365-mile stretch. From the northern coast going south the mountains push progressively closer to the coast limiting population growth and farming in the southernmost region.

Accordingly, Cannon Beach and its environs are essentially at sea level (and subject to tsunamis) and very amenable to the seaside tourism.

We will take Rte. 101 down the coast all the way to San Francisco. It is 2 lanes with an intermittent passing lane to leapfrog the slower traffic of campers, RV's, trailered outboard motor fishing boats, vintage VW buses, Subarus and logging trucks. The ubiquitous logging trucks are mostly extended bed trucks with an extension trailer that when stowed resembles a grasshopper or praying mantis. The pavement is wet. When these log-burdened trucks are hurtling downhill into a turn yawing towards you, there is a palpable fear that the multiple-ton log load is about to burst its bindings and spill into your path. So, get used to it.

Logging, commercial fishing, tourism and California retiree's drive the coastal economy. In addition to the logs being hauled on the highway as the Rte. 101 passes through timberland we come upon vast expanses of cleared forest extending high above, way below and alongside the roadway. After heavy-equipment cutting, the once-forested landscape is scared: a muddy, denuded yellow-brown battleground with scattered, dry logging debris and tree remnants. Albeit to the eye of this outsider, the clearing process, nevertheless, appears to be rational, staged and judiciously executed with abundant evidence of restoration, reforestation and new growth efforts.

Manzanita Neahkahnie Viewpoint

We come upon a vista point with a bird's-eye view of Manzanita. The view is obscured by smoke and fog but reveals a broad beach assaulted by relentless lines of surf and the mountain formations distantly beyond. On a clear day we would have had a spectacular panorama of the Nehalem Bay and its surrounding meadows. Timing is everything.

The Nehalem Estuary with its bay and wetlands initially pushes 5 miles inland until the Nehalem river forks and thins out. The Rte. 101 snakes around the bay before returning to the coast. The area is subject to winter, Pacific storm flooding. It is sparsely populated and dairy farming and tourism have replaced its earlier reliance on logging. Approaching the coast there are several pockets of recreational fishermen on the bay fully engaged in trolling for Coho and Chinook salmon.

Nehalem Bay

Driving south, we make a quick stop for a photo shot of Smith Lake which is really a slough just beyond the beach at Barview, a small community just north of the Tillamook Bay jetty inlet. The Tillamook estuary with its bay covers 9,200 acres and its fertile valley is dominated by the dairy farms that provide milk for the well-known Tillamook Cheese enterprise.

Smith Lake (Slough)

Our next stop is the Tillamook Cheese Factory and Visitor's Center. There is extensive expansion construction of the guest facilities underway; nevertheless, the unpaved parking lot is full of cars, trucks and RV's. The Center's structure is a large modern barn design with large windows. Ceramic dairy cows are exhibited along with dairy and cheese making displays and educational presentations oriented to the youngsters. It is standing room only at the ice creamery station and the retail cheese counter is three-deep.

Continuing south of Tillamook, Rte. 101 swings 5 miles inland from the coast linking a string of tiny pastoral communities named Pleasant Valley, Beaver, Hebo and Cloverdale. We drive through woodland and then the lush pastures supporting dairy production. The pastoral landscape of grazing meadows, buffering grass fields and hedges is verdant, isolated and calming.

Cloverdale Meadow

Next, Rte. 101 returns to the coast at Winema Beach where lush ocean meadows tumble to the beach sand. Winema ("woman chief") is a 2 mile strand that includes haystacks and shoreline caves. There is an abundance of wildlife (seals, bald eagles, deer). Beware of hightides. We note there are only 10 parking spots and no comfort facilities.

Following Winema, we then motor through a number of small beach towns on our way to Newport.

Winema Beach Meadow

In Newport, we are staying at the Hallmark Resort which is a large complex directly situated on the beach close to the popular summer resort, Nye Beach. The fog has lifted for a good hour and we enjoy some wine on the patio while watching late afternoon beachgoers strolling the beach. No one is in the water.

The fog returns with a passion at dinner time. We check out the popular Georgie's Beachside Grill which is oversubscribed so we opt for an alternative in the Bayfront District. We select Rogue Ales Bayfront Public House which is a no-frills gastropub offering a seafood menu and handcrafted beers in a waterman's, working-man's laid-back setting. Dinner consists of Dungeness crab cakes and several rounds of Rogue Seven Hop IPA beers. Unlike Georgie's, we are rubbing elbows with locals in their preferred dining locale.

SEPTEMBER 7, 2017: FLORENCE, SILTCOOS LAKE, COOS BAY AND BANDON.

Out early in the fog and mist in search of a Starbuck's for a cappuccino and a latte, I pull into a service station to gas up. Stepping out of the car and preparing to pump gas, I am immediately approached by an attendant who in no uncertain terms cautions me not to touch the pump as it would be a fineable offence for both me and the station owner. In a state of admonishment, I ponder whether this gentleman is obliged, after extensive gas pump operation and safety training, to obtain a state license to pump gas …and if he must submit to continuing education requirements. So now I know. What utter legislative nonsense (mandatory compliance removed January 1, 2018).

Newport, with a population of 11,000, relies on commercial fishing to drive its economy. It boasts an active water front and is the home of the renowned Oregon Coast Acquarium and the base for the National Oceanic and Atmospheric Administration and Hatfield Marine Science Center research vessels.

In an effort to find some photographic opportunities, although overcast, we return to the Bayfront District. The Bayfront faces the inner harbor which is crowded with a fleet of commercial salmon boats and pleasure yachts. Opposite the harbor are a line of tourist shops and eateries promoting local culture and industry. The area is noisy with the din of machinery from the hulking Trident Seafoods fish processing plant and cacophony of barking sea lions which have Francine quivering in the back seat. We skip the popular Underseas Garden exhibit. The persistent fog is oppressive.

Ghostly Piers: Newport's Bayfront District

Before heading out of town we swing by the Yaquina Bay Lighthouse situated in the Yaquina Bay State Park which straddles the inlet to Yaquina Bay. This light is one of two iconic lighthouses associated with Newport. It is not to be confused with the historic beacon and majestic (93 feet high) Yaquina Head Lighthouse north of Newport.

Yaquina Bay Lighthouse

Viewed from the State Park, I photograph the fog-bound outline of the Yaquina Bay Bridge looming over the Bay. Beyond the bridge is the silhouette Newport's Public Fishing Pier. The arch bridge was built beginning 1934 replacing a ferry service and features art deco finials atop the main piers at each end of the center arch span. It is the most recognizable of eleven major Oregon bridges designed by Conde McCullough. It towers 246 feet with 133 feet of clearance from the bay surface.

Yaquina Bay Bridge

Newport's Yaquina Bay is not to be mistaken as the location for the zany, impromptu fishing trip portrayed in the movie, "One Flew over the Cuckoo's Nest." Those scenes were shot in the mini 6-acre harbor of picturesque Depoe Bay lying about 10 miles north of here.

Our destination now is Bandon. As we motor south the landscape and industry is increasingly timberland. We cross the Siuslaw River at Florence halfway between Newport and Coos Bay. South of Florence is the Siltcoos Lake, the largest coastal lake in Oregon along with two other smaller sister lakes. It is a remnant of the Siuslaw River delta with a shallow depth of no more than 15 feet fed by freshwater tributaries. The lake supports abundant aquatic growth and is a popular recreational fishing venue for freshwater fishing and an occasional transient salt water specimen.

Pressing on we enter the northern tip of Coos Bay estuary which penetrates more than 5 miles inland to the Coos River tributary. Coos refers to the the major tribe that had inhabited this area for several millenia.

The city sits on a triangular peninsula oriented north-south which splits the bay into large bodies to the east and west. Coos Bay (16,000 population) is the largest city on the coast and is vibrant economically. The Marshfield District downtown projects an energetic, healthy and low-vacancy storefront image. There are historic buildings, theaters, shops, restaurants, galleries and parks. It is the hub for southeast Oregon that is powered by a collection, processing, milling and transiting center for the logging industry. There is an extensive railway and waterway infrastructure for transport of the timber-based commerce. The logging industry has clearly consolidated in Coos Bay.

Passing through Coos Bay we rapidly cover the 20 miles to Bandon. Bandon formerly a settlement for the Coquille tribe sits just inside the jettied ocean inlet for the Coquille River. The town of less than 4,000 has a small and compact center. We drive directly to our lodging, "Windermere on the Beach", south of town and arrive in a downpour. The lodging is quite spacious and sits behind dunes on a low bluff above the beach. After settling in we drive down to the village for dinner at Alloro Wine Bar and Restaurant. It is a limited seating venue serving Italian inspired dishes. We sat at the bar and were served by one of the owners who operates the restaurant with his partner and former spouse who is the chef. It obviously works as this meal ranks as one of the best of the trip. After dinner we stroll through downtown where most of the businesses have closed early as the town appears to be a retiree-populated, early-to-rise, early-to-bed haven. It has its appeal though smaller, less touristy or toney as Cannon Beach.

Pressing on we enter the northern tip of Coos Bay estuary which penetrates more than 5 miles inland to the Coos River tributary. Coos refers to the the major tribe that had inhabited this area for several millenia.

The city sits on a triangular peninsula oriented north-south which splits the bay into large bodies to the east and west. Coos Bay (16,000 population) is the largest city on the coast and is vibrant economically. The Marshfield District downtown projects an energetic, healthy and low-vacancy storefront image. There are historic buildings, theaters, shops, restaurants, galleries and parks. It is the hub for southeast Oregon that is powered by a collection, processing, milling and transiting center for the logging industry. There is an extensive railway and waterway infrastructure for transport of the timber-based commerce. The logging industry has clearly consolidated in Coos Bay.

Passing through Coos Bay we rapidly cover the 20 miles to Bandon. Bandon formerly a settlement for the Coquille tribe sits just inside the jettied ocean inlet for the Coquille River. The town of less than 4,000 has a small and compact center. We drive directly to our lodging, "Windermere on the Beach", south of town and arrive in a downpour. The lodging is quite spacious and sits behind dunes on a low bluff above the beach. After settling in we drive down to the village for dinner at Alloro Wine Bar and Restaurant. It is a limited seating venue serving Italian inspired dishes. We sat at the bar and were served by one of the owners who operates the restaurant with his partner and former spouse who is the chef. It obviously works as this meal ranks as one of the best of the trip. After dinner we stroll through downtown where most of the businesses have closed early as the town appears to be a retiree-populated, early-to-rise, early-to-bed haven. It has its appeal though smaller, less touristy or toney as Cannon Beach.

CHARLES ANDERSON

Bandon Harbor

SEPTEMBER 8, 2017: GOLD BEACH, REDWOOD NATIONAL AND STATE PARK AND EUREKA

The morning sun is rapidly burning off the fog. The flocks of squawking, frenetic and foraging seabirds with their breakfast now over have flown off.

The well-beaten trails through the beach brush immediately below our lodging are inviting us to hike to the ocean. Passing through the brush, we sink in above our ankles in the soft sand as we make our way through the dune line that gives way to a wide and all but deserted beach. The beach is littered with tidal detritus and shell remnants of early morning seabird banquets. The strand is roughly a mile long and is bounded by the Face Rock State Scenic Viewpoint seacliff overlook to the north and another Haystack Rock to the south. We hike north to rock formations and tidal flats just below the overlook. Face Rock (an indian legend inspired by the facial features of a human) is 2,000 feet off the beach; however, there are a collection of spindly towers and a single monolith about the size of a football field immediately off the bluff and approachable during low tide.

Seabird Morning Banquet Remnants

Kelp Sea Monster

Francine is fascinated by the kelp piles washed onto the beach and barks and romps frantically with a mix of fright while aggressively testing the kelp monsters for life and exhibiting amazement at these alien creatures. We approach the eroding monoliths which are poking out of the tidal flats. In the flats between the monoliths and the seacliff, a sand artist has fashioned a variety of rakes a swirling, asymmetric, a "yellow brick road" sand trail. A gaggle of tourists are admiring and audience-participating in the sand art. Karen and Francine gleefully joined in the small gathering as they troop on towards "Oz".

Sand Art at Face Rock Beach

We reverse course and pass along the dune line in the direction of the haystack at the south end of the beach. The wind and surf sculpted dunes are stabilized by tufts of grass resembling fescue but growing to heights of 4 feet. The dunes run as much as 100 yards inland from the tidal high point and give way to laurel woody scrub vegetation and, then, coastal pines on the bluffs overlooking the beach. Looking south towards the haystack there is a large tide pool serving as a vast soup bowl for a variety of dawdling seabirds.

Bandon Dune Grass

MOUNTAIN MEADOWS...OCEAN MEADOWS

Massive Bandon Haystack

Growing on the pines situated on the bluffs of the grounds where our cottage is located is a bearded plant curiosity reminiscent of the deep-south's Spanish moss.

Coastal Pines Draped with Spanish Mosses

We wrap it up in preparation for motoring on to the giant redwood county but on the way out of town a photograph of the

73

Coquille River lighthouse is a must.

Bandon has achieved some notoriety in the outside world by virtue of its world class golf course, "Bandon Dunes", which hosts pro golfing events. We didn't visit the golf course as Bandon itself, especially with clear skies, has been a delight with its natural wonders and small ocean village vibe.

Coquille River Lighthouse

Gold Beach Stacks

Heading south for about an hour to Gold Beach, the weather is cooperating and the scenery is no longer obscured by fog, smoke or a combination of the two. Just north of Gold Beach are a series of stacks jutting out of the ocean in sunny, daylight conditions.

We pull up on the northern heights of Wedderbum overlooking the Rogue River inlet. Presented below is a colorful blanket of 3-man, recreational, aluminum, outboard fishing boats trolling the inlet and extending into the estuary beyond the Bridge. We then cross the Issac Lee Patterson Memorial Bridge spanning the Rogue River. The bridge set back about 2,000 feet from the Pacific Ocean inlet. It has art deco motifs to include at each end prominent pylons of stepped vertical moderne elements with stylized Palladian windows with sunbursts.

This bridge is another one of eleven Oregon coastal bridges designed by Conde McCullough whose artwork we previously witnessed at the Yaquina Bay Bridge. These bridges replacing ferry services were constructed during the Roosevelt depression-era, public works campaigns during the 1930's and share a common inspiration, design and utility with that of their more majestic cousin found further down the coast, the Golden Gate Bridge.

Issac Lee Patterson Memorial Bridge

We immediately stop at the Port Hole Cafe for lunch just on the south shore of the Rogue River. I inquire about the fleet of fishermen stretched across the Rogue River and the hostess relates that this week is the height of the summer Steelhead Trout run. You literally could make your way across the river by leaping from boat to boat.

Dogs are not allowed in the dining area so we share a table in the corridor with Francine. We order up a Dungeness Crab Melt that turns out to comprise the most generous single serving of this delicate and delectable crab meat that we have experienced the whole trip.

Continuing south, we have now crossed into California and passed through Crescent City which has the dubious distinction of being tsunami-prone and actually suffered damages to boats, piers and moorings following the Sendai (Fukushima) Tsunami of 2011.

Roughly 15 miles south of Crescent City, the Newton B. Drury Scenic Parkway splits to the west from Rte. 101 and runs 10 miles through the Prairie Creek Redwoods State Park before reconnecting with the Rte. 101. Of course the stately redwoods are a magnificent site to behold, a first time for both of us. These are primeval, old-growth coastal giants that tower 300 plus feet and with diameters exceeding 20 feet. We dismount the car for a closer look. It takes some adjustment to balance yourself and crane your neck to view the full height of these colossal specimens. The thick stands at times block the sunlight. It is mind-boggling to contemplate that many of these redwoods are more than a thousand years old. This collection of giants is nirvana for professional botanists and tree huggers and awe-inspiring for your ordinary, semi-retired road-trippers.

Note Bene: About 20 miles north, in Jedediah Smith Redwood State Park on Mill Creek Trail, The Grove of Titans, discovered by redwood experts in 1998, is a 3-acre grove of redwoods that are some of the tallest trees on the planet. Kept mostly secret for decades since discovery, new trails, mostly elevated to protect vulnerable plants on the forest floor from human foot traffic, have been open for visitors since September 2021. The trail, under construction since 2019, was fully completed in July 2022.

CHARLES ANDERSON

Prairie Creek Redwoods State Park

Redwood Colonnade

The 14,000 acre Prairie Creek Redwoods State Park is jointly managed by California Department of Parks and Recreation and the National Park Service. The area now is a sanctuary for old-growth redwoods. It was originally exploited for gold mining but played out early in the 1920's at which time its owners began to contribute their land holdings to a park for protected status and public recreation. There is a visitor's center, hiking trails and camp grounds with a stunning, grassy meadow that regularly supports giant elk herds. The park was used for backdrop scenes in the movie, "Jurassic Park".

Roosevelt Elk Meadow

We complete the brief excursion through the park and motor on to Eureka (metro population 45,000). After the initial Gold Rush in the Sierra Nevada's east of San Francisco, a second round of prospecting took place in Northern California and Eureka came into being by virtue of easy ocean transport to the fields via Humboldt Bay. The gold quickly played out but the demand for lumber to meet burgeoning construction demands in San

Francisco and Eureka's proximity to prodigious redwood forests propelled it commercially to such heights that it was given the moniker, "Lumber Capital". Lumber is the major economic driver for Eureka but it is vulnerable to boom and bust cycles and has declined since the 1990's from Canadian and Southeast U.S. price competition. Fishing while secondary to lumber is a major industry producing half of California's commercial catch. Nevertheless, it also has contracted in response to regulatory, economic and cultural influences.

While Eureka's golden era has passed the city has done a remarkable job in restoring and maintaining its Victorian past. Its Old Town Eureka Historic District is a business district encompassing 3 blocks in from the bay-front and is chock full of vintage office facades and store fronts. The area appears to be busy with plenty of foot traffic and well maintained.

We are lodging close by in the "Carter House Inn". The Inn is actually a complex including hotel, restaurant, houses and a cottage which are renovations or replicas of the Queen Anne style popular in late 19th century California. The Inn's restaurant is closed for a private function so we drive into Old Town to explore and select a restaurant. We choose the Sea Grill for dinner. It is a large establishment with bar, dining room and banquet rooms. The menu is surprise ...seafood. The food is excellent and all the tables are filled with animated and boisterous patrons.

Carter House Inn Lodging

SEPTEMBER 9, 2017: EUREKA TO SAN FRANCISCO

Pink Lady

We are out in the early fog (again) for the next leg to San Francisco. Some picture taking first as there are several more remarkable Queen Anne specimens in the Old Town to experience.

First is the "Pink Lady" a classic Victorian built as a wedding gift by William Carson the lumber baron of the 1880's for his son. It has all the classical elements to include a turret, scalloped shingles, gingerbread exterior trim and sculpted wood accents. Of course, it is painted pink with white trim.

Across the street Carson built for himself the over-the-top and world famous Carson Mansion, a three story, eighteen room structure with a tower and basement. It was designed by the Newsom Brothers of San Francisco, well-known architects throughout California, and has become a local landmark. There are many interesting architectural points of view regarding the Mansion. It has many adornments such as wide porches with pillars, gables, turrets and cupolas. The structure now houses the Ingomar Club a private club of prominent locals with the principal mission of maintaining the Carson Mansion.

In departing Eureka, it is essential to comment on the people living on the streets. Notwithstanding efforts to restore the Old Town to its former glory there are pockets of street dwellers milling about, panhandling, open use of drugs, sleeping in the parks and using the public areas as restrooms. This condition is even more oppressive in San Francisco.

Ingomar Club

For the first 30 miles outside of Eureka, Rte. 101 follows the course of the Eel River and then its South Fork. We are traveling through considerable elevation changes and, accordingly, the drive twists and turns with the directional movement of the river bed. It is very scenic with breathtaking immense gorges followed by flat water with beaches.

This fork of the Eel River is the third largest river in California and extends for 105 miles inland to its source, Bald Mountain, in the Mendocino National Forest in Mendocino County. Until damming of the river took place in the 1920's, it had abundant runs of steelhead and salmon. These dams are due for removal in the near term with the plan to restore the fish habitat. Being from Southern California, the Eel River was an unknown; however, one understands why the locals would want to keep this natural treasure a secret. It has wild and scenic river designations from state and federal agencies and has a wilderness look and feel more like Colorado.

We stop for a photograph. From a bluff on the edge of the Humboldt Redwoods State Park there is the din of park goers frolicking in calm waters and on a serene beach below.

This forest setting goes into my memory bank as a candidate for a return trip to the Northern California wilderness. The waters are so calm and the beach so fresh and inviting that one imagines a day of family recreation that passes without any recollection of the time and the finale of an outdoor cookout. Only a handful of nature lovers have this treasure all to their own.

MOUNTAIN MEADOWS...OCEAN MEADOWS

South Fork Eel River Humboldt Redwoods State Park (Viewing East)

South Fork Eel River Humboldt Redwoods State Park (Viewing West)

We continue downhill out of the redwoods through isolated hamlets into the farming communities of Mendocino County. We pass through the tiny communities of Leggett, Willits, Ukiah and then the wineries begin to emerge. Next is Sonoma County and the wide valley supporting the bountiful mosaic of world class vineyards. Gliding through Santa Rosa, it appears to be in the midst of a significant housing construction boom along with the attendant traffic disruption from the widening of Rte. 101 and the erection of traffic sound barriers.

Within a month wind-driven forest fires devastate parts of this community. The Tubbs Fire destroyed over 5,600 structures and resulted in almost two dozen losses of life. The origin of the fire was failure of a private electrical system adjacent to a residential structure.

The remaining leg to San Francisco zips by. Passing through Marin county and once over the Golden Gate and into town, we head straight up Gough Street to Pacific Heights to Lafayette Park to stretch our legs and to give Francine a respite from the ride from Eureka. The park is full of weekenders soaking up the splendid weather: sunbathers, dog walkers, unleashed dogs, frisbee gamers, picnickers and children. From this prominence looking downtown towards the Bay, there is a new structure nearing completion on the skyline. The Salesforce Tower at 1,070 feet is soon to be the tallest building in San Francisco.

Sales Force Tower

Spreckles Mansion

San Francisco Bay from Pacific Heights

We walk the perimeter of the park and stop at Octavia Street to ponder the Speckles Mansion a major San Francisco landmark. This immense beaux arts chateau was built in 1912 by a 19th Century sugar baron, Claus Spreckles, for his wife Alma who is a worthy personality known as the "great-grandmother of San Francisco". The mansion is currently the home of the prolific author Danielle Steel. What an urban contrast to the rural Eel River valley.

Below, the Bay, looking towards Sausalito, is relatively devoid of commercial and recreational boating traffic for such a textbook sailing day of sun and wind.

After a healthy walk in the Heights searching out a restaurant from the past, Jackson Fillmore Trattoria, which turns out to be closed until 5:00 p.m., we drive over to Union Square and check into the Sir Francis Drake.

Once settled in, we enjoy a drink at the Drake's main bar which is overcrowded with a large throng gathered for a wedding.

With Francine in tow, we stroll down to a jam-packed Union Square which is bathed in the late afternoon glow of the sun. The streets are choked with tourists, tour buses, shoppers and panhandlers. After circulating the Square and a short stretch of Market Street we head up Grant Street towards Chinatown. At Bush Street we happen upon the Café de La Presse and decide to stay for dinner and several "French 75" cocktails. After dinner we climb the hill to Chinatown and window shop the store fronts before returning to the hotel.

Francine Abuzz at Café De La Presse

SEPTEMBER10, 2017: UNION STREET AND SAN JOSE

We checkout of the Drake and drive to Perry's on Union (street) for breakfast. We want to do a short hike at Balboa Park but it is Sunday and the streets on the way are almost impassable as they are cordoned off for neighborhood pedestrian festivals and clogged with families, baby carriages and pets. Balboa Park is absolutely overrun with weekend park denizens and there is not even a postage stamp on which to park. We throw in the towel and decide to continue to San Jose where we are meeting some new relations for dinner.

In San Jose we tour around the Santa Clara University campus and along the Alameda with its toney neighborhoods and grand houses. Later that evening we have a pleasant get together with our new relations and a delightful Italian dinner at Paesano's.

Tomorrow, we embark for a six-hour jaunt back to Southern California.

CHARLES ANDERSON

Bridalveil Fall Zoomed-In

ABOUT THE AUTHOR

Charles Anderson

Residing in Corona Del Mar, CA, the author is a retired Administrator for an orthopedic surgical medical group. Charlie is a management and financial professional having prior career positions in international finance in Washington, D.C. and New York City. He has this book and two prior published credits utilizing his considerable bank of business writings. A graduate of the University of Maryland he also has a Master's degree from Harvard. He served as a U.S. Army Artillery 1st Lieutenant in West Germany during the Vietnam Era.

BOOKS BY THIS AUTHOR

Provence In September

September in Provence is a travelogue in journal form with 80+ photos of a 4-week vacation in Provence. The vacation was composed and organized on-our-own rather than submitting to a packaged tour via bus or boat cruise. It is an account of the travel experiences of eight aging American baby boomers day tripping Provence with a side trip to Barcelona from a base in Aix-en-Provence (Aix). The base lodging is a rustic, third story apartment with no elevator in the heart of the historic district of Aix near the Place Richelme which hosts a daily al fresco farmers market. Aix, in a sunny and warm climate, itself possesses an abundance of attractions, café life, shopping, a significant university population and a popular, central gathering place, the Cours Mirabeau. Within an hour plus drive from Aix lie Arles, Avignon, Nimes, St. Remy, Marseille, Cassis, Uzes and the Luberon villages of Fountain du Vaucluse, Gordes, Menerbes, Bonnieux, Apt and Loumarin. Within two hours are St. Tropez, Grasse, Cannes, Nice and Monaco. Barcelona is a five-hour cross country run on the autoroute.

The journal communicates the pleasures of traveling in southern France and details the recollections, color, some history and highlights of each of the Provencal towns visited. In Barcelona the Rambla and the Gothic Quarter sights and tapas are featured in some depth. Moreover, the journal describes the daily experiences and encounters of foreign travel that present one with out-of-one's comfort zone, experiences and refreshingly new perspectives and insight on custom and culture. The former relates to negotiating narrow, unfamiliar streets while the latter is expressed in testing one's language skills in the markets and restaurants. Lastly, the photos capture the essence of our travels.

Paris In September

Imagine renting a flat in central Paris and indulging yourself with a weather-friendly, month-long exploration of this world-renowned tourist mecca and seat of French art, culture, commerce, government and history. Paris in September transports you through this indulgence with daily journals with photos of this dream vacation. Visit the iconic sites such as Notre Dame de Paris, the Louvre, Versailles, the Champs-Elysees and the Eiffel Tower. Take the Metro to the Cemetery Pere Lachaise to view the gravesites of Jim Morrison and Oscar Wilde. Attend a special exhibition to admire the Seventeenth Century canvasses of Caravaggio at the Museum Jacquemart-Andre. Catch the Bullet Train to London. Browse the sumptuous Galeries Lafayette on Boulevard Haussmann or a rolling market in the Butte-aux-Cailles neighborhood. Find a front-row café seat on the Rue Montorgueil and enjoy a Belgian blond beer while watching the Parisians out for a Saturday evening. Experience this travelogue and, then hopefully inspired, plan your very own getaway.

Made in the USA
Columbia, SC
05 August 2022